20 LUCRATIVE BUSINESS YOU CAN VENTURE INTO AS A WOMAN OR HOUSEWIFE OR A STAY AT HOME MUM.

Step by step guides to financial empowerment course for women who want to thrive.

Jenny Pearl.

Copyright © [Jenny Pearl] [2023]

Table of content

10.Homemade Food Business

11.Personal Care Products

12.Handywoman Services

13.Childcare Services

14.Fitness Coaching

15.Pet Sitting/Dog Walking

16.Interior Design Consultation

17.Online Reselling

18.Gardening Services

19.Photography

20.Life Coaching

These ideas cater to a wide range of interests and skills, making them accessible for

women, housewives, and stay-at-home
moms looking to start a business from home.

Introduction

In a tranquil suburban neighborhood, where white picket fences and well-manicured gardens were the norm, there lived a woman named Emily. She was the embodiment of the modern homemaker, a dedicated wife, and a loving mother. Yet, beneath her seemingly ordinary life, a burning desire for something more simmered.

It was one of those quiet Sunday mornings, the kind that seemed tailor-made for introspection. Emily gazed out of her kitchen window, sipping her morning coffee, and wondering if there was a way to blend her roles as a woman, a housewife, and a mother with the fervor of an entrepreneur.

As the sunlight filtered through the window, an idea dawned on her like a ray of hope. It was a realization that would set the course for an extraordinary journey.

Emily's story is not unique. It's a story of countless women, housewives, and stay-at-home moms who yearn for financial independence and a purpose beyond the household chores. It's a tale of resilience, creativity, and unwavering determination.

In the following pages, we will unveil not just Emily's story but also 20 Lucrative Business Ideas that can transform the lives of women like her, and like you. These are stories of women who turned their passions, skills, and dreams into thriving businesses from the comfort of their homes.

From the allure of e-commerce to the satisfaction of crafting handmade wonders, the thrill of writing and the joy of baking, this guide is a treasure trove of possibilities. It's an invitation to dream big, embrace change, and craft your own success story. Whether you are a woman seeking to redefine your role, a housewife looking to contribute financially, or a stay-at-home mom with untapped potential, this is your journey of empowerment.

So, fasten your seatbelt, and let's embark on this inspiring adventure where household dreams meet entrepreneurial realities. Welcome to "20 Lucrative Business Ideas You Can Venture Into as a Woman, Housewife, or Stay-at-Home Mom," your gateway to a world of limitless opportunities.

Factors to consider before starting a business

Before embarking on a lucrative business venture as a woman, housewife, or stay-at-home mom, several critical factors must be considered to ensure success and sustainability:

1. Market Research: Thoroughly analyze the market to identify demand, competition, and potential customers. Understanding your target audience is vital.

2. Business Plan: Create a detailed business plan outlining your goals, strategies, and financial projections. It serves as a roadmap for your venture.

3. Budgeting: Calculate startup costs, ongoing expenses, and expected revenue.

Ensure you have the financial resources to cover these.

4. Time Management: Assess your availability and create a schedule that accommodates your business alongside household responsibilities.

5. Legal Structure: Decide on the appropriate legal structure for your business, such as sole proprietorship, LLC, or corporation.

6. Licensing and Permits: Check local regulations and obtain the necessary licenses and permits for your business.

7. Branding and Marketing: Develop a brand identity and marketing strategy to promote your products or services effectively.

8. Skills and Training: Invest in education or training if required to enhance your skills and knowledge in your chosen field.

9. Support System: Seek support from family and friends or join entrepreneurial networks to access guidance and mentorship.

10. Risk Assessment: Identify potential risks and have contingency plans in place to mitigate them.

11. Home Office Setup: Create a conducive workspace at home with necessary equipment and technology.

12. Scalability: Consider the scalability of your business, allowing for future growth and expansion.

13. Work-Life Balance: Strive for a healthy work-life balance to prevent burnout and maintain personal well-being.

14. Adaptability: Stay flexible and adapt to changing market conditions and customer preferences.

15. Networking: Connect with other entrepreneurs, attend industry events, and build a strong professional network.

These factors are essential for any woman looking to venture into a profitable business while managing household responsibilities. Success in entrepreneurship often hinges on careful planning and a proactive approach to addressing challenges.

Chapter one

Online Retail

Online retail is a lucrative business opportunity for women, including housewives and stay-at-home moms, seeking to generate income while balancing household responsibilities. The digital age has opened up countless avenues for entrepreneurship, and here's why online retail is an attractive choice:

1. Flexibility: Managing an online store allows you to set your own hours, catering to your family's needs. You can work during nap times, after bedtime, or whenever you have spare moments.

2. Low Overhead: Unlike traditional brick-and-mortar stores, online retail requires minimal upfront investment.

3. Diverse Product Selection: You can sell a wide range of products, from handmade crafts to niche goods. Choose items that align with your interests and expertise to increase your passion for the business.

4. E-Commerce Platforms: User-friendly e-commerce platforms and marketplaces like Etsy, eBay, Amazon, and Shopify make it easy for beginners to create and manage their online stores.

5. Market Reach: The internet allows you to reach a global audience, increasing your customer base and potential sales.

6. Work from Home: Running an online retail business can be managed from the comfort of your home, reducing commute time and childcare costs.

7. Learn and Grow: Online retail provides a great learning experience. You can acquire marketing, sales, and business management skills that can be valuable in the long run.

As a woman, housewife, or stay-at-home mom, online retail empowers you to pursue your entrepreneurial dreams and contribute financially to your household, all while being present for your family. With dedication and a strategic approach, this business endeavor can be not only lucrative but also fulfilling.

Chapter two

Blogging And Content Creation

Blogging and content creation offer an exciting and potentially lucrative business opportunity for women, including housewives and stay-at-home moms. Here are compelling reasons to consider this path:

1. Flexibility: Blogging and content creation allow you to work on your own schedule, making it a perfect fit for managing family responsibilities. You can write, create videos, or design graphics when it suits your lifestyle.

2. Passion-Driven: You can choose to focus on topics that genuinely interest you, whether it's parenting, cooking, travel, or a hobby. Sharing your expertise and experiences can resonate with a like-minded audience.

3. Low Startup Costs: Starting a blog or YouTube channel doesn't require significant upfront investment. With a computer and internet connection, you can create high-quality content from home.

4. Monetization Opportunities: As your content gains an audience, you can monetize it through advertising, sponsored posts, affiliate marketing, or selling digital products, such as ebooks or online courses.

5. Learning and Skill Development: Blogging and content creation will sharpen your writing, video editing, and marketing skills, providing valuable personal and professional growth.

6. Potential for Passive Income: Over time, your content can generate passive income, allowing you to earn money while you focus on other priorities.

By becoming a content creator, you can turn your passion and knowledge into a thriving online business. It offers women the chance to balance family life while pursuing their entrepreneurial aspirations and achieving financial independence. With determination and consistency, blogging and content creation can be a rewarding venture.

Chapter three

Handmade Crafts

Handmade crafts represent an appealing and potentially lucrative business opportunity for women, particularly housewives and stay-at-home moms. Here are compelling reasons to consider this creative path:

1. Artistic Expression: Crafting allows you to express your creativity and passion, making it a fulfilling way to channel your talents and hobbies into a business.

2. Unique Products: Handmade items are often cherished for their uniqueness and personal touch, which can attract a niche market willing to pay a premium for one-of-a-kind creations.

3. Low Overhead: Starting a craft business typically requires minimal investment. You

can work from home, reducing costs associated with renting a physical space.

4. E-Commerce Platforms: Platforms like Etsy and social media make it easy to showcase and sell your crafts to a global audience, reducing the barriers to entry.

5. Customization: You can offer customized items, allowing customers to personalize products according to their preferences, adding value to your offerings.

6. Learning and Growth: Crafting can be an ongoing learning experience, improving your skills and opening doors to new techniques and artistic abilities.

7. Support Local and Sustainable: Handmade crafts often align with eco-conscious consumers looking to support local artisans and sustainable practices.

By leveraging your creative talents, you can turn your love for crafting into a thriving business venture. Handmade crafts offer the opportunity to generate income while nurturing your passion, all while maintaining a work-life balance that's crucial for women managing household responsibilities. With dedication, marketing savvy, and an eye for quality, this pursuit can become both lucrative and fulfilling.

Chapter four

Freelance Writing

Freelance writing stands as a lucrative business opportunity ideally suited for women, including housewives and stay-at-home moms. Here's why it's an appealing choice:

1. Flexible Schedule: Freelance writing allows you to work on your terms, fitting tasks around family responsibilities. You can write during nap times, evenings, or whenever you have spare moments.

2. Low Entry Barriers: You need little more than a computer and internet access to get started. No expensive equipment or office space is required.

3. Diverse Writing Opportunities: Freelancers can explore various niches, from blog posts and copywriting to technical

documentation and creative writing. This versatility means you can choose subjects that align with your interests and expertise.

4. Remote Work: You can work from home, eliminating the need for a daily commute and allowing you to maintain a balanced lifestyle.

5. Growing Demand: The digital age has led to a surge in online content creation, which means a consistently high demand for quality writers.

6. Learning and Growth: Freelance writing is an opportunity to refine your writing skills, build a portfolio, and learn about different industries and topics.

7. Income Potential: With experience and a strong portfolio, you can earn a substantial income. Many freelance writers successfully support their families through their work.

Freelance writing offers women the means to channel their creativity and passion into a profitable venture while maintaining family responsibilities. As you build your client base and reputation, it can become a fulfilling and lucrative business.

Chapter five

Social Media Management

Social media management is a thriving and potentially lucrative business venture for women, including housewives and stay-at-home moms. Here's why it's an enticing opportunity:

1. Flexibility: Managing social media accounts allows you to work from home on a schedule that suits your family's needs. You can post content, engage with followers, and analyze data during your free moments.

2. Low Overhead: The startup costs for a social media management business are minimal. All you need is an internet connection and a computer or smartphone.

3. In-Demand Skill: As businesses increasingly rely on social media for marketing and customer engagement, social

media managers are in high demand. Your services can help companies maintain a strong online presence.

4. Niche Specialization: You can focus on industries or niches that align with your interests, expertise, or previous experience, allowing you to work on content you're passionate about.

5. Remote Work: Social media management can be done remotely, providing the flexibility to balance household responsibilities.

6. Learning Opportunities: You'll gain valuable skills in content creation, marketing, and data analysis, enhancing your marketability.

7. Income Potential: As you build your client base and reputation, social media management can provide a steady income, and you can even scale your business over time.

By venturing into social media management, you can transform your social media savviness into a rewarding career. It offers the chance to combine your passion for online interaction with entrepreneurship, contributing to your family's finances while embracing the flexibility and work-life balance you need as a woman, housewife, or stay-at-home mom. With dedication and the right strategies, this can become a lucrative and gratifying business.

Chapter six

Virtual Assistant

Virtual assistance presents a lucrative and flexible business opportunity that aligns perfectly with the lifestyles of women, including housewives and stay-at-home moms. Here's why it's an appealing choice:

1. Flexibility: As a virtual assistant, you have the freedom to set your working hours, allowing you to balance your family's needs while providing essential support to businesses.

2. Low Startup Costs: You don't need significant upfront investments, as you can start with just a computer and internet connection, working from the comfort of your home.

3. Varied Services: Virtual assistants offer a wide array of services, from administrative

tasks and email management to social media management and customer service. You can tailor your services to your skills and interests.

4. Remote Work: Being a virtual assistant means you can work from anywhere, eliminating the need for a daily commute and childcare costs.

5. Growing Demand: Businesses and entrepreneurs often seek virtual assistants to handle their non-core tasks, which ensures a consistent demand for your services.

6. Learning Opportunities: This career provides a chance to enhance your skills in areas like organization, communication, and time management.

7. Income Potential: With the right clients and skillset, virtual assistants can earn a substantial income, allowing you to contribute financially to your household.

Virtual assistance enables women to leverage their organizational and administrative skills to build a thriving business. As you gain experience and expand your network, this opportunity can become both lucrative and fulfilling, offering a satisfying work-life balance that suits your family's needs.

Chapter seven

Online Tutoring

Online tutoring is a highly lucrative and flexible business venture that offers women, including housewives and stay-at-home moms, the chance to share their knowledge and make a meaningful impact while managing their household responsibilities. Here's why it's a compelling choice:

1. Flexible Schedule: Online tutoring allows you to set your own hours, making it easy to work around your family's needs. You can choose to tutor during nap times, evenings, or weekends.

2. Low Overhead: The startup costs are minimal, mainly consisting of a computer, internet connection, and educational materials.

3. Diverse Subjects: You can offer tutoring services in a wide range of subjects, capitalizing on your expertise or passions.

4. Remote Work: Tutoring can be done from home, eliminating the need for a physical workspace and reducing commuting time.

5. High Demand: The demand for online tutoring is consistently growing, especially with the rise of remote learning and the need for personalized education.

6. Empowering: As a tutor, you have the chance to empower students, help them achieve their academic goals, and build their confidence.

7. Income Potential: With the right marketing and qualifications, online tutoring can be a lucrative venture. Many tutors charge competitive rates, making it financially rewarding.

Online tutoring is a fulfilling way to blend your knowledge and skills with entrepreneurial aspirations, all while prioritizing family life. Whether you have expertise in math, science, language, or any other subject, this business offers a rewarding opportunity to make a significant income and a positive impact on your students' lives.

Chapter eight

Consulting

Consulting can be an excellent and flexible business opportunity for women, including housewives and stay-at-home moms. Leveraging their expertise, experience, and skills, they can offer valuable services in various fields. Here are some lucrative consulting avenues to consider:

1. **Digital Marketing**: With the increasing demand for online presence, offering digital marketing consulting services can be profitable. Women can assist businesses in creating effective online strategies, managing social media, and optimizing their web presence.

2. **Parenting and Childcare**: Stay-at-home moms can leverage their parenting experience to provide parenting advice and childcare consulting. This can

include running parenting workshops, offering childcare tips, and helping other parents navigate the challenges of raising children.

3. **Nutrition and Wellness**: Women who have a background in nutrition and wellness can offer consulting services in this field. They can guide clients on healthy eating habits, exercise routines, and overall well-being.

4. **Home Organization and Interior Design**: Many women excel in creating beautiful and organized living spaces. Consulting on home organization and interior design can be a profitable venture.

5. **Tutoring and Educational Consulting**: Women with teaching experience can offer tutoring services or educational consulting to help students excel academically.

6. **Career Coaching**: With their own career experiences, women can assist others in achieving their professional goals by offering career coaching and resume building services.

7. **Event Planning**: Event planning and coordination is another area where women's organizational skills can shine. Consulting on event management and design can be a lucrative business.

Consulting businesses allow women to leverage their skills and passions while maintaining flexibility to balance family responsibilities. These ventures can be started from home, making them even more accessible and convenient for housewives and stay-at-home moms looking to contribute financially to their households. With dedication, the potential for success in these fields is substantial.

Chapter nine

Event Planning

Event planning can be a lucrative business venture for women, including housewives and stay-at-home moms. This profession offers the flexibility to balance family responsibilities with a thriving career. Here's why it's an excellent choice:

1. Flexibility: Event planning allows you to set your own hours and take on as many or as few clients as you can manage. This flexibility is crucial for women who want to prioritize family life.

2. Creativity: Many women excel in creative endeavors, and event planning is a platform to showcase your artistic talents. You can design and execute weddings, birthday parties, corporate events, and more, giving clients memorable experiences.

3. Networking: Building a strong network is essential in this industry. As a woman, you have access to diverse social circles, enabling you to connect with potential clients and vendors more effectively.

4. Low startup costs: Event planning doesn't require significant upfront investment. You can start small, gradually building your portfolio and investing as your business grows.

5. Work from home: Much of the planning and client communication can be done from the comfort of your home, minimizing the need for a physical office.

6. Emotional intelligence: Women often possess excellent interpersonal skills and emotional intelligence, which are invaluable in understanding and meeting clients' needs.

By offering a blend of creativity, flexibility, and strong interpersonal skills, event planning can be a profitable and fulfilling business for women, allowing them to achieve financial independence while managing their household responsibilities.

Chapter ten

Handmade Food Business

Starting a handmade food business can be a lucrative and fulfilling venture for women, including housewives and stay-at-home moms. Here are some compelling reasons why this is a fantastic opportunity:

1. Culinary Skills: Women often excel in the culinary arts, and many have treasured family recipes and cooking traditions to draw upon. Your cooking skills can become your biggest asset.

2. Flexibility: A handmade food business can be tailored to fit your schedule. You can prepare food during your free time, such as when children are at school or napping, giving you the flexibility to manage both work and family responsibilities.

3. Low Overheads: Operating from home or a small commercial kitchen, your business can keep overhead costs low, making it financially viable to start and scale gradually.

4. Unique Offerings: Homemade foods often have a unique and authentic flavor that sets them apart from mass-produced alternatives. This uniqueness can be a strong selling point.

5. Local and Online Markets: You can sell your handmade food locally at farmers' markets, through food delivery services, or even online through your website or social media platforms.

6. Niche Markets: Specializing in a particular type of cuisine, dietary preference (e.g., gluten-free, vegan), or specific product (e.g., artisanal jams, baked goods) can help you target niche markets and stand out.

By turning your passion for cooking into a business, you can generate income while doing something you love. With dedication and effective marketing, a handmade food business can be a fulfilling and profitable venture for women, offering financial independence and the ability to manage household responsibilities.

Chapter eleven

Personal Care Products

Creating and selling personal care products can be a lucrative and empowering business venture for women, including housewives and stay-at-home moms. Here's why it's a compelling opportunity:

1. Demand for Natural and Handmade Products: Many consumers are seeking natural, chemical-free, and environmentally friendly personal care products. As a woman, your understanding of these preferences can be a valuable asset in crafting and marketing such items.

2. Customization: You can tailor your products to meet specific needs and preferences, such as skincare, haircare, or aromatherapy, offering customers a personalized experience.

3. Low Start-up Costs: Beginning at home or a small workspace, you can minimize initial investments and gradually expand as your business grows.

4. Online Sales and Marketing: With e-commerce platforms and social media, you can reach a broad audience without the need for a physical store. Online sales allow you to manage your business from home.

5. Creativity: Women often excel in creating aesthetically pleasing and high-quality products, which can set your brand apart from mass-produced alternatives.

6. Ethical and Sustainable Practices: Many consumers are concerned with ethical and sustainable product production. You can align your business with these values, appealing to a conscious consumer base.

Personal care products encompass a wide range of items, including skincare, bath and body products, cosmetics, and more.

Leveraging your creativity, knowledge of natural ingredients, and marketing skills, you can establish a profitable business while balancing your family responsibilities. This venture allows women to achieve financial independence and express their creativity in a thriving market.

Chapter twelve

HandyWoman Services

Offering handywoman services can be a lucrative and empowering business venture for women, including housewives and stay-at-home moms. This field presents various advantages for those looking to enter it:

1. Skill Set: Many women possess skills in home repairs, maintenance, and DIY projects. These capabilities are highly sought after in the handywoman services industry, where you can excel and showcase your expertise.

2. Flexibility: This business allows you to set your own schedule, taking on jobs as they fit into your daily routine and family responsibilities.

3. Low Overheads: Starting as a one-woman operation, you can keep overhead costs low. You only need essential tools and equipment to get started.

4. Growing Demand: The demand for reliable handywomen is on the rise, with many customers preferring to work with female professionals who offer attention to detail and great communication skills.

5. Empowerment: As a handywoman, you break traditional gender roles, empowering yourself and inspiring other women to pursue careers in non-traditional fields.

6. Wide Range of Services: Handywoman services can encompass a broad spectrum of tasks, including plumbing, electrical work, carpentry, and general home repairs. You can diversify your skills and take on various projects.

By leveraging your skills, work ethics, and determination, starting a handywoman services business offers women the opportunity to achieve financial independence while managing family responsibilities. You can carve a niche for yourself in a growing market, delivering valuable services and building a successful career on your terms.

Chapter thirteen

Childcare Services

Starting a childcare services business can be a rewarding and profitable venture for women, including housewives and stay-at-home moms. Here's why it's a fantastic opportunity:

1. Expertise: Women, especially mothers, often have a natural knack for caring for children. Your experience as a parent equips you with the skills and understanding needed to excel in this field.

2. Flexibility: Running a childcare service from home allows you to create a flexible schedule that accommodates your family's needs. You can provide care while still being there for your own children.

3. Low Overheads: The initial investment for a home-based childcare service is

relatively low, primarily involving childproofing your home and acquiring age-appropriate toys and materials.

4. High Demand: The demand for quality childcare services is consistently high. As more parents work full-time, the need for trustworthy and nurturing childcare providers remains strong.

5. Safety and Trust: Parents often feel more comfortable leaving their children in a home environment with a caring woman who understands their needs.

6. Niche Specialization: You can choose to specialize in certain age groups, offer bilingual or educational programs, or cater to children with special needs, giving your business a unique selling point.

By leveraging your maternal instincts and dedication, you can create a thriving childcare services business that not only generates income but also allows you to make a positive impact on the lives of the children you care for. This venture provides a fulfilling path to financial independence while managing household responsibilities.

Chapter fourteen

Fitness Coaching

Becoming a fitness coach is an excellent and lucrative business option for women, including housewives and stay-at-home moms. Here's why this career path is so appealing:

1. Passion for Health: Many women have a genuine passion for health and fitness, making them well-suited for coaching and motivating others to adopt healthier lifestyles.

2. Flexibility: As a fitness coach, you can design your schedule to accommodate your family's needs. This flexibility allows you to balance your career with household responsibilities.

3. Minimal Startup Costs: Starting a fitness coaching business often requires minimal

upfront investment. You can begin with your expertise, a few pieces of exercise equipment, and an online presence.

4. Online Training: The rise of online training and virtual coaching has made it easier for women to reach a broader audience, without the need for a physical gym or studio.

5. Empowerment: This profession allows women to inspire others and help them achieve their fitness goals, leading to a sense of empowerment and fulfillment.

6. Market Demand: The demand for fitness coaching is consistently high, as more people recognize the importance of leading a healthy lifestyle. You can tap into a growing market.

By sharing your knowledge and passion for fitness, you can establish a profitable career as a fitness coach. It provides an opportunity for financial independence while allowing you to manage family responsibilities effectively. This venture not only supports your well-being but also empowers you to inspire and change the lives of others for the better.

Chapter fifteen

Pet Sitting / Dog Walking

Starting a pet sitting and dog walking business is a lucrative and flexible venture that women, including housewives and stay-at-home moms, can excel in. Here's why it's a compelling opportunity:

1. Love for Animals: Many women have a natural affinity for pets and enjoy their company. This passion can be the foundation for a successful pet care business.

2. Flexibility: Pet sitting and dog walking allow you to set your own schedule. You can provide services while your children are at school or during your free time, making it compatible with family life.

3. Low Overheads: The initial costs are minimal, mainly involving marketing

materials and possibly insurance. You don't
need a dedicated office space.

4. Growing Demand: As more people own
pets, the demand for reliable pet sitters and
dog walkers is on the rise. Families often
prefer the personalized care and attention
that a dedicated caregiver can provide.

5. Emotional Connection: Caring for pets
can be emotionally fulfilling and offer a
sense of companionship, making it a
rewarding and enjoyable business.

6. Community Engagement: A local pet care
business often thrives through
word-of-mouth recommendations, allowing
you to engage with your community and
build a strong client base.

By providing quality care for pets, you can
establish a profitable business while
balancing your household responsibilities.
This venture offers the opportunity to
achieve financial independence, pursue a

passion, and create a flexible career that allows you to enjoy the companionship of furry friends while earning an income.

Chapter sixteen

Interior Design Consultation

Interior design consultation is a lucrative and creatively fulfilling business option for women, including housewives and stay-at-home moms. Here's why it's an appealing choice:

1. A Keen Eye for Design: Many women have a natural talent for aesthetics and creating beautiful living spaces. Your innate sense of style can be a valuable asset in the interior design field.

2. Flexible Work Arrangements: Interior design consultations can often be scheduled to suit your lifestyle, allowing you to balance family responsibilities with your passion for design.

3. Low Startup Costs: Starting small and gradually building your client base keeps

initial costs relatively low. You can work from home and grow your business at your own pace.

4. Customization: Offering personalized design solutions, you can cater to individual client preferences and create unique, tailored spaces that reflect their personality and needs.

5. Growing Demand: The demand for interior design services remains strong as people seek to enhance their living environments. A well-designed space can have a significant impact on a person's well-being.

6. Strong Networking: As a woman, you can leverage your social network to build connections with potential clients and local suppliers, which is essential in the interior design industry.

By combining your design skills with creativity, effective communication, and an understanding of your clients' desires, you can build a thriving interior design consultation business. This venture offers the opportunity to achieve financial independence while indulging your artistic passion, all while managing your household responsibilities.

Chapter seventeen

Online Reselling

Online reselling is a highly lucrative and flexible business that women, including housewives and stay-at-home moms, can venture into successfully. Here's why it's an attractive opportunity:

1. Low Start-up Costs: Beginning as an online reseller requires minimal upfront investment. You can start with items you already own or source affordable products to resell.

2. Flexible Schedule: Online reselling allows you to work at your convenience, fitting around your family's needs. You can list and manage items when it suits you.

3. Wide Product Range: You can sell a variety of items, from clothing and accessories to electronics, home decor,

vintage goods, or handmade crafts, catering to your interests and expertise.

4. E-commerce Platforms: Online marketplaces like eBay, Amazon, Etsy, and platforms like Poshmark and Mercari make it easy for women to reach a broad audience without the need for a physical store.

5. Scaling Potential: You can scale your business as you become more experienced, potentially turning it into a full-time income source.

6. Networking Skills: Women often excel at building connections, which can be beneficial in sourcing products, establishing partnerships, and growing your reselling business.

Online reselling provides women with an opportunity to combine their entrepreneurial spirit with flexibility. It allows you to generate income while managing household responsibilities. The reselling world is vast, offering ample room for creativity and customization to suit your individual interests and market niches. By dedicating time and effort, online reselling can become a lucrative and empowering business venture.

Chapter eighteen

Gardening Services

Starting a gardening services business can be a profitable and rewarding venture for women, including housewives and stay-at-home moms. Here's why it's a fantastic opportunity:

1. Love for Nature: Many women have a deep appreciation for gardening and the environment. This passion can be the foundation of a successful gardening services business.

2. Flexible Schedule: Gardening allows you to set your own working hours, providing the freedom to balance family 6commitments while pursuing a career.

3. Low Startup Costs: Starting small with basic gardening tools and equipment keeps initial investments minimal. You can grow

your business gradually as you gain more clients.

4. Growing Interest: As more people seek green and sustainable living spaces, the demand for skilled gardeners is on the rise. Your expertise can be a valuable asset in meeting this demand.

5. Creative Expression: Gardening services offer a platform for creativity and design. You can transform outdoor spaces into beautiful gardens, showcasing your skills and imagination.

6. Community Involvement: A local gardening services business often relies on word-of-mouth recommendations, allowing you to connect with your community and establish a strong client base.

By sharing your love for gardening and horticultural knowledge, you can create a thriving business while maintaining household responsibilities. This venture provides an opportunity to achieve financial independence, pursue your passion, and contribute to the beauty of outdoor spaces. Gardening services can be both lucrative and fulfilling for women with a green thumb.

Chapter nineteen

Photography

Photography is an enticing and profitable business for women, including housewives and stay-at-home moms, who have a passion for capturing moments and expressing their creativity. Here's why it's an excellent opportunity:

1. Creative Outlet: Many women possess a keen eye for aesthetics and a love for capturing moments. Photography provides a creative outlet for self-expression.

2. Flexible Schedule: As a photographer, you have the flexibility to schedule photo shoots around your family's needs, making it ideal for balancing work and home life.

3. Low Entry Barriers: You can start small with basic equipment and gradually invest in more advanced gear as your business grows.

An initial investment in cameras and editing software is typically all that's needed.

4. Diverse Specializations: Photography offers various niches, such as portrait, wedding, event, landscape, or product photography. You can choose a specialization that suits your interests and skills.

5. Online Presence: In today's digital age, you can create an online portfolio, use social media, and offer your services through websites, reaching a broad audience without the need for a physical studio.

6. Empowerment: Becoming a photographer empowers women to build a business from their artistic talents, achieve financial independence, and inspire others with their creativity.

Photography is a profession that combines artistry and entrepreneurship, allowing you to turn your passion into a profitable career.

With dedication, a good eye for detail, and effective marketing, you can create a thriving photography business while managing household responsibilities. It's a creative and lucrative path to financial independence and personal fulfillment.

Chapter twenty

Life Coaching

Embarking on a career as a life coach is a lucrative and rewarding business venture for women, including housewives and stay-at-home moms. Here's why it's an enticing opportunity:

1. Empathy and Communication: Women often excel in empathetic listening and effective communication, essential skills for guiding and motivating individuals to achieve their goals.

2. Flexibility: Life coaching offers the flexibility to set your own working hours, making it easier to manage family commitments while pursuing a fulfilling career.

3. Low Overheads: Starting a life coaching business typically requires minimal initial

investment, primarily involving training and marketing materials.

4. Growing Demand: In a fast-paced world, people are seeking guidance to navigate challenges and reach their full potential. The demand for life coaches is on the rise.

5. Empowerment: Empowering others to achieve their aspirations is not only professionally rewarding but also personally fulfilling.

6. Varied Specializations: Life coaching encompasses a wide range of specializations, from career coaching to wellness and relationship coaching, allowing you to focus on areas you are passionate about.

Life coaching enables women to combine their natural abilities for empathy and guidance with professional training to create a profitable business. It offers the opportunity to achieve financial independence while making a meaningful impact on the lives of others. By dedicating your time and skills, you can help people reach their full potential while successfully managing your family responsibilities.

Conclusion

In conclusion, there are numerous lucrative business opportunities that women, including housewives and stay-at-home moms, can successfully venture into. These opportunities not only provide financial independence but also empower women to pursue their passions and contribute to their family's income while balancing household responsibilities. Here are some key takeaways:

1. **Flexibility is Key**: Many of these business options offer the flexibility to create your schedule, allowing you to prioritize family life while building a career. This adaptability is a valuable asset for women who want to achieve a work-life balance.

2. **Low Startup Costs**: Most of these businesses can be started with minimal initial investments, making them accessible

to those with limited resources. As you grow, you can reinvest in your business gradually.

3. **Passion and Skills**: Leveraging your passions and skills is a common theme among these opportunities. Whether it's a love for cooking, a green thumb, an eye for design, or a knack for coaching, your natural talents and interests can become the foundation for a successful business.

4. **Market Demand**: The demand for many of these services remains strong, offering a consistent client base. From personal care products to pet services and life coaching, these businesses cater to growing and evolving consumer needs.

5. **Online Platforms**: The rise of e-commerce and online platforms has made it easier than ever for women to market their products and services. You can reach a broader audience without the need for a physical storefront.

6. **Empowerment and Fulfillment**:
These ventures empower women to take control of their financial future, turning their interests into profitable careers. The satisfaction of building a business, helping others, and finding personal fulfillment is invaluable.

It's important to remember that success in any business endeavor requires dedication, hard work, and effective marketing strategies. But with determination and a clear vision, women can achieve financial independence, personal fulfillment, and a successful career while managing the responsibilities of a household.

The world of business is open to all, and these opportunities highlight that women can pursue their entrepreneurial dreams, make a significant impact in their chosen fields, and inspire others to do the same. As these women-led businesses thrive, they continue to break barriers and redefine traditional roles, contributing to a more inclusive and diverse business landscape.